SILENT SCREAMS
SILENT JOY

SILENT SCREAMS
SILENT JOY

POEMS AND WRITINGS

MARIJEAN HALL

SILENT SCREAMS SILENT JOY
POEMS AND WRITINGS

iUniverse books may be ordered through booksellers or by contacting:

iUniverse
1663 Liberty Drive
Bloomington, IN 47403
www.iuniverse.com
844-349-9409

Because of the dynamic nature of the internet, any web addresses or links contained in this book may have changed since publication and may no longer be valid. The views expressed in this work are solely those of the author and do not necessarily reflect the views of the publisher, and the publisher hereby disclaims any responsibility for them.

Any people depicted in stock imagery provided by Getty Images are models, and such images are being used for illustrative purposes only.
Certain stock imagery © Getty Images.

ISBN: 978-1-6632-0888-0 (sc)
ISBN: 978-1-6632-0889-7 (e)

Library of Congress Control Number: 2020918040

Print information available on the last page.

iUniverse rev. date: 10/23/2020

To Carol, a wise and wonderful spiritual advisor and renowned psychologist whose words formed the foundation of my surviving.

"You did what you needed to do to survive. And thank God you did, for you are here today for us to love."

Foreword

I have had the opportunity to work with Marijean professionally as her therapist over three years. During that time, I have learned many lessons from Marijean. Throughout our work, I have been continually impressed by her courage, determination, and spirit of joy, even in the face of many traumas and hardships. Her indomitable spirit is an inspiration to all of us. These meditations on the "tears of things," as well as the hope herein, can guide us all in our journeys.

Julia A. Ahrens, PhD

Introduction

Have you ever tried to find the beginning or the end of a tightly wound ball of yarn or perhaps a knot you need to untangle? Well, I have. And writing this introduction for you has been a similar experience. It has been made difficult by the fact that my writings were not done to be published but to help me survive physical and emotional pain.

I am a survivor of sexual, mental, and physical abuse. My medical history is complex and extreme. In 2011, I had an episode of severe intestinal pain, then major cognitive dysfunction and chronic fatigue. It wasn't until 2013 that I was diagnosed with Lyme disease. And it wasn't until 2015 that I was diagnosed with moderate to severe PTSD—*the perfect storm*.

I started writing in 2014, and three people very devoted to me encouraged me to publish those poems. I was skeptical, but I did do a little research. I finally decided that publication was not my goal—too difficult and too public. Five years later, I became convinced that perhaps my writings might be valuable to others. I researched self-publishing and began the process of looking at my writings in a whole new way, not just as my way to cope with my reality but as my way to connect with others who have also been through their own perfect storm.

My perfect storm in a nutshell:

My life from the outside looks pretty amazing. I have lived in thirteen states and in sixteen cities/towns and have attended six universities. I have had ten jobs and have owned my own company. I have a bachelor's in political science and a master's in public administration, and I have completed coursework toward a master's in education. I was featured on the cover of *Money* magazine as the subject of the lead article. I have been the catalyst for nationwide public health campaigns that decreased and/or eliminated diseases. I was awarded the 3M Innovator Award, and many of my accomplishments have been covered nationally in the print media and on television.

However, the toll of years of abuse and several major physical crises finally felled me. I have had fourteen hospitalizations and more than fifty ER visits; I have seen over forty doctors and have received numerous differing diagnoses; and I have been prescribed fifty different medications. I spent all my savings. I lost the ability to do the things I once loved. I almost lost my soul.

The following pages illustrate that I am writing my way out of the darkness. It's a journey, from darkness to a light at the end of the tunnel. I know there are many others who have taken this journey. I also know some are having difficulty finding that light. I hope sharing my journey will give you hope if you can't find the light. If you, too, can finally see and believe in that light, then perhaps our shared journey will give us even more strength, along with the faith that life is a gift we can now enjoy fully.

It is important to me that these writings help you find your voice. So, after each writing, I have provided a blank page titled "Your Voice." Write one word; comment on my writing; or give voice to your inner feelings. Don't judge your voice or self-edit. I learned this lesson well! Open up your heart and write.

If you believe that *Silent Screams, Silent Joy* will be of value to others, then please let them know.

Contents

Six Notes, Three Words— A Father's Love, A Child's Terror

It came on suddenly, these night terrors that froze my heart and stifled my voice.
So terrifying. It would take me hours to reach out to my parents.
Creeping one small step at a time,
Leaving my room and seeking the light from downstairs,
I would enter the light and seek the comfort of my parents.

Night after night my dreams were filled with devil worship and scenes from a movie,
A movie I should never have seen.
In it was a little boy whose first thought, *What is happening?*, was a dream because no one heard his voice.
A horror of aliens kidnapping all the adults,
Returning them to earth, but no longer human.
His dream was reality, and he was left alone.

My parents, disturbed, listened to me and comforted me, but no amount of comfort in the light would extinguish the terror once I was back in the darkness of my room.

It was the rich baritone of my father's voice singing the chorus from "Song of the Volga Boatmen"—a mournful song springing from the oppression of the Russian people—that quelled the images.

I heard my father's voice singing the chorus over and over again, as I still hear now.
He was sitting next to the bed in the dark, sometimes reaching over to touch my face.
Why that chorus? Why that song?
Where had he heard that song and why would he choose to sing that chorus over and over again?
Its cadence, his voice, his patience and love, all captured in six notes and these lyrics:

> Yo, heave-ho!
> Yo, heave-ho!
> Once more, once again, still once more,
> Yo, heave-ho!
> Yo, heave-ho!

Note: Listen to "Song of the Volga Boatmen" by Paul Robeson on YouTube.

Your Voice ...

I'm Nobody. Are You Nobody Too?

The dark reality of depression.
A life spliced together with short-term solutions
For unsolvable problems.
Pain of a magnitude nobody should have to endure
For a moment, a day, let alone a lifetime,
Combined with the inability to manage the simplest task.
A voice that screams out into the night but fades into the darkness.
The pain has stolen who I am with only the faint memory that I was somebody.

I am nobody. Are you nobody too?

A voice and a soul silent to everyone but me.
Fear and helplessness burden those who love me.
They cannot turn me into somebody again.

Your Voice ...

Groundhog Day

I'm not going to bed tonight—
A declarative sentence.
Why? you might ask.
Because each day is just like the day before.
Pain begins within minutes of waking up.
Several hours of trying to diminish the pain.
Fingernails holding on to a narrow cliff,
Going back to sleep to hide from the pain,
Knowing it may or may not get better.
Finally, after four or more hours of this tortuous
dance with the devil,
I can answer a call, send an email, breathe
deeply.
No guarantee the pain, which I choose to call
the devil, won't grab me
And begin the dance again.
So if there is no morning, then there is no
beginning and no end.
Groundhog Day does not exist,
So maybe I will not exist in this never-ending
dance.

Your Voice ...

Boiling Blood

Don't be put off.
This is not a poem about cauldrons of blood boiling.
Well, it might be,
But it's not a scene out of a satanic movie.
It is about me.
The room is like a cold storage room,
A tightly sealed space.
Being bone-tired and struggling to stay awake,
I take my pills,
Tuck my furry puppy in,
Rub his tummy,
And go to sleep.

Like a thermostat turned up to one hundred degrees,
From within it begins.
I can feel the heat, immediately starting in my chest,
Rise quickly.
Then miraculously I fall asleep again, a dark sleep, no dreams.
Cold and wet,

Soaked in sweat that runs down my back,
I wake up startled,
Lying in a pool of water.

I rise quickly.
I have slept only four hours—not time to start
the day.
I drink cool water
And return to bed, switching to the dry side,
Heat rising again.
A dark sleep falls on me as before,
Only to feel the cold and wet drip from the back
of my neck,
Hoping, but knowing
The early signs of dawn are not there.

Your Voice ...

No More Tears

Dry eyes may have an underlying medical cause.
I say it is a warning sign that I have no more
tears.

Like a desert, I am totally devoid of water.
Sand, grit, wind, and heat have wiped away my
tears.
I cannot cry out in pain, sorrow, or anger.

Staying within,
My tears evaporate,
Leaving me depleted.
What you see is a mirage
Born of that human need to cry.

Your Voice ...

One More Day

One more day of pain that burns through my
body like a bullet intent on killing me.
One more day of a moment-by-moment choice,
whether I can do the simplest thing.
One more day of robbing Peter to pay Paul,
deciding what I can pay or not pay.
One more day of not doing things that bring me
joy and laughter, putting off my dreams.

One more day. One more day. One more day.
A refrain lived for more days than I can count,
my having ceased to count many days ago.
One more day and then there will be no more
days,
No more days.

Your Voice ...

Two Stones

Two stones,
Cold,
Round,
Pushed up against an opening,
Foreboding,
Ubiquitous,
Hidden within—a secret.
Timeless,
Universal.
If told, humankind would reel,
Paralyzed,
Terrified.
Joining hands across the world,
Moving,
Struggling,
Pushing the two stones and revealing the secret,
Cold,
Round,
Back into place, escaping the truth again.

Your Voice ...

The Perfect Medicine

A wicked night reigniting a deep mistrust for a friend.
A dream so real I could feel, smell, and taste the food being offered
And feel the haughtiness and "I win" attitude of a dear friend.
She has a weakness—men.
A deep-seated need to win a man at any cost, even if that cost be a friend,
And then subordinate herself and all around her to the needs of that man.

That was the beginning of my day.

Shaking that dream off is possible with the light of day,
But it resides permanently as another betrayal.
Anxiety born of fear that I can't trust anyone, not even God,
Begins in the pit of my stomach,
Rising to a level that grips me.

I pace, talk to myself, and rub my fingers through my hair, my heart racing.
Ah, Ativan. One doesn't work, so I take two and wait the requisite twenty minutes.

I try to distract myself by going through my morning routine:
Coffee, two cups,
A treat for my fluffy pup.
Fifteen minutes later, I fix my pup breakfast,
Counting the seconds until I can breathe.

I've smoked all my cigarettes by 9:00.
I realize the Ativan is not working,
So I distract myself with making the bed, picking up the bedroom, and dressing.
Then I make a desperate run to buy cigarettes.

At 10:00 I take a clonazepam,
My go-to drug for anxiety.
Twenty minutes of watching the horrors around us on the news.
I am breathing again,
All thanks to those magical pills.

I realize that not only can I breathe, but also I have no pain.
I am lost, without purpose.
No pill can fill that void.

Nothingness.
I fill it with a fine wine and my favorite foods.
I accomplish little, but I do make some social arrangements,
Something I rarely do.
Pain, remember?
Unpredictable and debilitating.
What gave me the notion that I could commit?
Maybe the pills, the wine, and my favorite foods.

Your Voice ...

Letter to God I

Dear God,

It's been awhile since I've written. It seems my days are an exercise in survival. I sleep to stave off the pain and discomfort so I may seek solutions and be there for my loved ones.

I am physically and emotionally wasting. Wasting—a failure to thrive. My gifts are being wasted, my time is being wasted, my capacity to love is being wasted. What a waste to you and my service on this earth.

Like a leper, I feel cast out, hiding in a cave, afraid to go out without a mask to hide my anguish.

God, please stop my wasting. Let me thrive. My life is given over to you and your Son, Jesus Christ.

Your servant,
Marijean

Your Voice ...

Letter to God II

Dear God,

I appreciate your invitation to live. I have started in at times, and it is wondrous. I regret I will not be able to attend the event at this time because I am consumed with the event called "surviving." The event has had a long run, although I have begged to be replaced as the star or to have the director call it a day. The program has received rave reviews with adjectives like *heroic* and *courageous*, or in one actor's words, "You are a fighter."

These words, though heartening at the moment, do nothing to sustain me for long. I am a person on life support, spending most days merely breathing in and out. Unlike many, I am not brain-dead; much to my dismay, I am fully aware, sensing everything—the touch of my puppy's fur; the wrinkles in the sheet; the nauseating smell or repugnant thought of food; the burning pain that never ends; the sight of a woman once beautiful, now bloated and exhausted, and whose eyes, once brilliant, are now dull.

To accept your invitation, I must accept that you have a plan. Like Sarai, I have grown impatient; the promises seem to fade. I have no joy or comfort, though I have prayed for these things, sometimes over and over again. Jesus, your Son, I was told, would walk in the garden with me. I am not walking now at a steady pace, but I stop and look to see if he may be behind me, or I stare ahead to see if he is waiting. Realizing he is not there, I turn back to take whatever comfort is a phone call away.

Your child,
Marijean

Your Voice ...

My Child's Soul

My child's soul is at stake.
Innocent,
She stares quietly inside a circle.
Familiar faces, even mine,
Waiting, waiting, waiting
For me to recite a familiar prayer,
The Lord's Prayer.
The terror rises.
My mind goes blank.
The cord grows tighter around my throat.
I tear at it,
Reach out desperately to grab her hand.
No words.
No hand.

Note: For forty-two years, I could not recite the Lord's Prayer. Then one day, in a circle of familiar faces, we began to say the prayer. The words flowed out from me, as they have continued to do every day since.

Your Voice ...

Conscience

That human element that keeps us from crossing that dark line in the sand,
It's turning gray.
How can she love me?
My holier-than-thou opinion of myself as a mother.
Yes, I didn't leave—I did show up—but my, my, what a price she paid.
Bad men, bad women, bad decisions.
Never a moment when she could feel safe or know I was sane.
A fog of insanity covered neatly by brilliance, humor, and kindness.

Your Voice …

Ghosts

Like Scrooge, who on Christmas Eve saw ghosts
of the present, the past, and the future,
I see those same ghosts:
Men I abused and who abused me,
Alcohol that I abused and which abused me,
Never-ending needy people whom I really
needed.
The present,
Full of emptiness except for the never-ending
ringing of my phone,
Not calls from friends or family but robocalls,
which
Never stop trying to get me to pick up the phone.
Hiding from them, and from the pain I live with
daily;
Slipping off my shoes and sliding beneath the
covers;
Turning off the phones, knowing that no one who
cares will call,
Only those who want to take something I don't
have.
I realize that I don't have anything
Except for my home, which

Soon could be taken too.

That is my present.
There will be no future when the present is nothing.

Your Voice ...

Empty Self-Portrait

If I were asked to draw a self-portrait,

The outline of my face would create an empty
space.
My features have long faded away.
Items would appear, not features—
Pictures of things that create my portrait.

Clonazepam, a drug that keeps the madness
away and stops my skin from exploding.
Dr. Pepper, a taste that I crave that makes the
pain easier to swallow.
Hot fudge sundaes, a reward for surviving
the day.
Coffee with cream, a tool in awakening some of
my senses.
My fluffy dog, whose fur, gently stroked, brings
a simple joy and a brief moment of peace.

How can this happen,
An insidious and constant loss of self?

Your Voice ...

Confusion

"I don't know what's right. I don't know what's wrong. I don't even know what's going on."

That's a memorable line from a burned-out drug addict,
Reverend Jim—
You remember, from *Taxi*—

Who spoke that universal truth:

We're asked too much
And we hear too much and
Know too little,
So we fear too much.

Constant noise, 24/7,
Explodes into confusion,
Madness.
Focus on self.
Me, me, me.
No us, us, us.

Your Voice ...

A Promise Made, a Promise Unkept

"I will find you wherever you are, and we will grow old together."
Those are the most loving words ever spoken to me.
Although our lives would take different paths, I would be loved as I grew old.
A man, a self-proclaimed devil, with an angel's touch.
A sex addict, bipolar, and alcoholic.
A genius, a truth teller, a predator.
A drug dealer, a marine, an undercover agent.
A devoted father and son, a friend, a lover.
A lifelong risk-taker, driven by self-hatred and a fear of living.
A man who made every cell in my body explode,
Creating an opening no other had found.

I waited and hoped he would keep his promise.
A Shakespearean-like love affair.
Since then, I no longer believe in promises,
So many of them unkept.

Your Voice ...

A Drop of Cream

Black so black, not light,
Served in a small espresso cup,
Not to be sullied by cream,
The blackness to be sipped.

In my drinking of that first sip, the blackness
seems to merge into the fluid crimson red of
my blood.
Moving through my veins, it slowly fills my organs.
Then my body begins to sink into itself.

Like mixing more and more espresso,
Brown into crimson red,
A drop of cream
Appears in the middle of the cup.

Slowly, so very slowly, sinking into the blackness.
No lightening of the edges, only the small place
where the cream dropped.
A tiny espresso spoon, sitting precariously on
the saucer,

Can, with circular movement,
Lighten the darkness.
And when sipped, it begins slowly, so slowly, to
pull me into the light.

Your Voice ...

Alive

Alive.

Why? Fear that I will never see my Ollie again or my daughter and grandchildren.
I could take him with me into the vortex of darkness or light.
Like Dorothy clutching Toto, my dog and I may end up in a poppy field or a castle full of flying monkeys.
As in the movie, the poppy field is a metaphor for heroin; I see it literally,
Running through a field of brilliant red poppies with an azure-blue sky,
Sunlight streaming down on me as I run not to or from anything.

Free, free at last.

No pain, no loneliness, no suffering.

Alive.

Your Voice ...

Kaleidoscope

A small twist of the globe.
A cacophony of brilliant color.
Intricate designs.
Keep twisting.
Seamlessly,
Another cacophony of color appears,
Intricate designs.

Who thought of such a thing?
Who designed it?
Who made it work?

I want to meet that person.
It was centuries ago.
He could tell me how his mind works,
And I could create in my mind
A never-ending kaleidoscope.

Your Voice ...

Snow Globe

If you shake a Christmas snow globe,
Then set it down,
Crystalline flakes of snow so large, so moist,
Fall and dissolve, gone,
As if they were never there.
In that globe,
Pine trees and Christmas lights
Create a path for a father and his little girls'
Christmas Eve walk home,
Three hearts held together by two hands.
Quickly, too quickly, the snowflakes become fewer,
And they are home,
Letting go of their hands.
The door opens,
And the snow globe needs to be shaken again.

Your Voice ...

The Holy Spirit Got Me

The words just rolled off my tongue as if I were
a preacher man.
The unlikely young listener hanging on to every
word,
Writing what I said on Post-its,
Like hallelujahs at a revival meeting.

My words—born out of frustration with the world.
No longer striving for excellence,
Being desperate,
Hearing the word *hope* too often without any
action,
Having encountered a service provider who was
not providing service,
Rather a disservice.

A twenty something woman given the
responsibility
But no tools to solve the problem.
The desperate sound in her voice to quell my
frustration.

For fifteen minutes I went on about the revelations in my life,
Including the day I said to someone "I am not desperate and will never be desperate."
Free, free at last.

The man who changed my life with the words "Hope is not a strategy,"
And the inner glow of seeing, hearing, or knowing excellence in the world and in yourself—like melted gold streaming through your veins.
First you feel a mellow warmth, heating up, ending with a burst of glory,
Like a preacher man leaving a woman wanting to hear more and to feel the glory.

Your Voice ...

An Angel's Place

When twilight slowly but sweetly comes,
And when the lights dim,
A heartbeat away are the soft folds of a resting
place,
A special place
Created just for you, my love.
In those folds are all the magic places a child
needs,
The rhythmic beat of a mother's heart,
Warm breath like wisps of sunny air,
Arms that seem to wrap you in liquid gold.

In that place you will grow.
Your hands and feet will push to be free
And reach up to touch the soft petals of skin
That lay just beyond your reach,
But they slowly move, so slowly meet.

The shadows grow darker
And your eyes heavier,
Retreating into the far realms
Where angels fly on wings of doves.

Your Voice ...

Hands Holding Mine

One so small,
So light, but firm.
An artist's hand
Holding tight,
Not out of fear
But out of love,
Shooting visions—
Princesses and unicorns,
Colored pink and purple—
Into my heart.

The other so strong,
So grounded,
So willing to grab hold,
Not out of fear
But out of love,
Shooting visions,
Steadying my hands on the wheel,
The calm amid the storm,
Colors of rich brown and blue
Pouring into my heart.

Your Voice ...

The End

The lights begin to dim.
The curtain drops.
The theater goes dark.
The play is over.
The last page has been read.
The last words have been written.
My battle to survive is over.
I won.

The end.

Your Voice …

In Gratitude

First and foremost, I am grateful to God for giving me the gift of writing; to devoted friends and family, old and new; and for the courage to take on the task of creating a book.

Second, I am grateful to my parents, who created in me a love of words, reading, and self-expression.

Three very dear people are responsible for this book's being published. My writings were hidden in my computer when a few were shared with my niece, Michelle Troxclair, a brilliant spoken-word poet, writer, and performer, who said I should publish them. This was in 2014 or 2015. I spent about two hours researching and talking to one person, and then I decided not to publish. I was too insecure and felt that publishing would be too personal with too much exposure. That is what kept me from pursuing what Michelle had suggested.

Probably the most unrelenting and encouraging person in my life is my therapist, Julia Ahrens,

PhD. When I told her I was considering publishing some of my work, she exploded with enthusiasm and kept after me. We were looking at target audiences and at first did not envision a book. My sister, Cenith Hall-Tibbs, took it to the next level, maybe two, by suggesting a universal value. I don't remember when or how, but all of a sudden it became a book.

Special gratitude goes to those who have given their time and talents to producing *Silent Screams, Silent Joy*: my sister, whose encouragement to write the book and whose thoughtful suggestions and writing have held me together during this process; Sue Tullipano, my friend and colleague whose talents and emotional support have taken the pieces and made them into a book; Nancy Bare, whom I have known since kindergarten, who has provided insight throughout the years and insight into this book; and Mary Ackerman, a childhood friend whose love of literature and writing provided that "forest for the trees" insight and who provided me with some great editing.

Another group of people who read some of the writings and provided valuable insights consists of Marcia Goldenstein, friend of fifty-five years; Don Brown, a new friend who has become a constant in my life in Kansas; and Ethan Collins, a young man whose comments were very insightful, making me see the book in a different way.

Although they were not directly involved in the book or my writings, I have to mention dear friends who have been steadfast throughout my life or most of my life: Cindy Lauterbach, whom I can't remember not knowing; Jan Amundson, a friend of fifty-five years who has laughed with me, danced with me, advised me, and stood up for me; and Waveny Mason, who was my work-study student in 1987, along with being an employee, a subcontractor, and a friend, who provided unqualified love for these thirty-three years.

Not too many people get adopted at seventy, but I did, by the Collins family. I was hospitalized in August or September of 2019, and a young man, Justin Collins, was my nurse. He wanted to stay in touch. It wasn't very long before his mother wrapped her arms around me and brought me into her loving family.

But perhaps my greatest gratitude goes to my daughter, Lauren Mullen. She has kept me safe and loved and has given me three adorable grandchildren, Maggie, Brennan, and Callan, who shine a light in my life every day.

God bless all of you.